THE
COMPLETELY
UNOFFICIAL
RIVER CITY
QUIZ BOOK

D0270426

THE COMPLETELY UNOFFICIAL RIVER CITY QUIZ BOOK

Paul English

Black & White Publishing

First published 2011
by Black & White Publishing Ltd
29 Ocean Drive, Edinburgh EH6 6JL

1 3 5 7 9 10 8 6 4 2   11 12 13 14

ISBN: 978 1 84502 359 1

A CIP catalogue record for this book is available from the British Library.

Typeset by RefineCatch Limited, Bungay, Suffolk
Printed and bound by CPI Group (UK) Ltd, Croydon, CR0 4YY.

Contents

Acknowledgements

Thanks for patience and research to: Jean Hamilton, Alasdair Baird, Brian Hamilton, Anne Marie Nimmo, Steve Hendry at *Daily Record* and *Sunday Mail* plus Karen Higgins and Roy Templeton at BBC Scotland. And to Dr Joan Perry and Geoff Nolan for timely dictation shifts. Special thanks to *River City* cast members past and present for giving up their time to help: Morag Calder, Allison McKenzie, Colin McCredie, Tony Kearney and the truly encyclopedic Tom Urie. See you for a pint down the Ship . . .

Introduction

IN 2001, Angela Dewar, my then boss at the *Daily Record*, gave me a special project. 'They're making a soap opera in Scotland,' she said. 'It's going to be like *EastEnders* in Glasgow. I want you to cover it.'

Ten years later, I've followed every cough and spit on the tarmac of Montego Street, watching the faces come and go with the tides of the Clyde on the banks of River City. I've been one of hundreds of thousands who regularly tune in across Scotland to catch up with the residents of the country's most famous fictional city suburb. From the Maliks to the Murdochs, the murders in the boat yard to the mayhem in Moda Vida, The Tall Ship shenanigans and the crisis coffees in the Oyster Café, I've followed it through good times and bad.

Now, as the soap approaches its ten-year anniversary, I've cast my eye back over the years and drawn up this collection of quiz questions covering everything from the first words spoken to what they put in Gina's buns. It's the only pub quiz they'll never have in The Tall Ship. So pull up a pew and we'll do it ourselves. Mine's a pint of pretend beer.

Paul English, *Daily Record* TV Critic, Summer 2011.

THE
QUIZZES

River City People

How well do you know your riverside regulars?

1. Which Scottish acting legend plays battleaxe Molly O'Hara?

2. Michael Mackenzie played camp hairdresser Robbie's boyfriend. But what was the character's name?

3. Neil McNulty plays which dodgy businessman?

4. Former Taggart star Colin McCredie played Nick Morrison. Was he a) a politician b) a joiner c) a train driver?

5. If Theresa is Shellsuit Bob's mum, who is his dad?

6. Which Dundee-born former *Corrie* hunk played Innes Maitland?

7. Which tousle-haired crimper is played by Gary Lamont?

8. Councillor Alex Judd was played by the real life brother of the actress who played Sharon McLaren from Arran. Name him.

9. And what is his big brother Martin's connection to the soap?

10. Which character did *Titanic* star Ewan Stewart play in *River City*?

11. What was Daniel McKee's wife's name? a) Fi b) Leigh c) Marianne

12. Name the unlucky in love character played by June Brogan.

13. Monica Gibb played which character? a) Lawyer Fi b) Barmaid Betty c) Nun Norma

14. Who played Shirley's best mate Viv Roberts?

15. What character did Scots beauty Kirsty Mitchell play when she appeared in 2008?

16. Sean Brown and Anthony Martin played which pair of brothers whose father was killed?

17. Polish actor Pavel Douglas played Patrick Johnston who formed an alliance with Archie Buchanan. Was he: a) a gangster b) a lawyer c) a coal man?

18. Julie Duncanson, who starred in BBC comedy *Velvet Soup*, played which controversial multiply-married character?

19. Homophobic cop DI Whiteside came on board to investigate DCI Hunter's death, but who played this rogue cop?

20. Which widowed mother of two did Jenny Ryan play?

For answers, please turn to page 101

3

Consider yourself ready to move in to Shieldinch if you can answer this lot . . .

1. Name both actresses who have played Jo Rossi.

2. Junior actor Adam Khan played which son of a character played by two different people?

3. Which famous Scottish newspaper agony aunt got a mention during a domestic spat between Jimmy and Scarlett in 2007?

4. Bob was engaged to, and nearly married, Charlie. But what was her surname? a) Chalk b) Nicholas c) Drummond

5. Who plays Deek?

6. Who plays Shellsuit Bob?

7. When Shellsuit Bob was written out due to the actor who plays him having fallen ill, where had he gone?

8. Name the actress who plays Scarlett.

9. Which flame haired *River City* actress has also been a singer in 1980s band Sophisticated Boom Boom?

10 Who has played Raymond Henderson since the show's beginning?

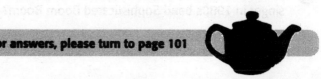

For answers, please turn to page 101

5

Clydeside Coupling

**Love makes the world go round – especially
on Tuesday nights on BBC1.**

**How well do you know the lives and loves of
the *River City* regulars?**

1. Shellsuit Bob proposed to Zara Malik from the top of a
   a) cherry picker b) JCB c) bin lorry.

2. Name the single mum who dumped Shellsuit Bob and
   stole his cash.

3. Father Michael became embroiled in a messy two-
   way split for his affections between which mother and
   daughter?

4. When Tina delivered the ultimatum to Eddie 'It's either
   Scott or me' which one did he walk out of The Tall Ship
   with?

5. Which of Roisin's sisters had an affair with Marty?

6. Who did Gina end up having an affair with behind Murray's
   back?

7. Which unlikely pair ended up locking lips during a game of
   spin the bottle in the students' flat?

8. Name Malcolm's late wife.

9. Just as Andy and Gabriella were about to get married what did Ruth do?

10. When Charlie snogged Nicole Brodie what didn't he know about her?

11. Leyla married Michael Brodie but where was her character from?

12. Which one of the following has never been Amber's boyfriend? a) Rory b) Lee c) Fraser d) Scott

13. Big Bob's girlfriend Tattie came from which country?

14. Where did Tattie and Big Bob meet?

15. Name Nick Morrison's wife.

16. Which teenager had a crush on councillor Nick?

17. Which Shieldinch copper did Ruth date?

18. PC Harry Black was played by Carter Ferguson. He was also one of the stunt men on *River City*. True or false?

19. Shellsuit Bob has never been married. True or false?

20 Alice Henderson cleaned up her act and returned in 2011 to marry Lewis Cope in a civil ceremony at Glasgow University. True or false?

**For More Clydeside Coupling,
continue directly on to the next quiz.**

For answers, please turn to page 101

More Clydeside Coupling

They're not shy, this lot. More matters of the flesh from the famous City streets . . .

21 Hogmanay 2010 – which two unlikely lovebirds finally snogged?

22 Which bloke did Rory snog in 2008? a) Scott b) Shellsuit Bob c) Nathan

23 Manu and Scott became a couple in 2008, but how did Scott try to put Manu off his scent early on?

24 Who stole Iona's knickers from her washing line?

25 Which Adams cheated on her boyfriend with Ewan Murdoch?

26 Who abandoned his vocation for Kelly Marie?

27 Who gave Marty an STD?

28 Which flame haired beauty had an affair with DI Whiteside to Scott's disgust?

29 Who did Jamie Hunter have teen relations with?

30 Name Roisin's American beau.

31 Billy Davies snogged Shirley Henderson, his ex-wife's mum, after his on/off romance with Tina Hunter. True or false?

32 Who did Bob's girlfriend Charlie lose her virginity to at a party? Bob or Liam?

33 Scarlett made a play for Father Michael, but who did she turn to for a one night stand when he rejected her?

34 When he was skelped on the head with the urn containing his dad's ashes, who was Archie having an affair with?

35 Alice snogged Shellsuit Bob, but that wasn't her only controversial winch. Who was the other one with?

36 Zoe ended up in an uneasy relationship with which authority figure in her life?

37 Who did Vader fall for when he was married to Hazel?

38 When he split with Della, who did Billy Davies end up in a relationship with?

39 Who did cop Eddie Hunter have an extra-marital relationship with?

40 Which alcoholic was Lewis Cope going out with when he was diagnosed HIV positive?

For Clydeside Coupling Continued, proceed directly on to the next quiz.

For answers, please turn to page 102

Who's surprised there are so many relationships blossoming – or withering – around Shieldinch? What else is there to do?!

41 Who did Dr Marcus get engaged to?

42 Raymond and Roisin were once married. True or false?

43 When Billy ran up gambling debts who did he make his wife sleep with in an *Indecent Proposal* style storyline?

44 Which character turned up decades after he seduced Alice when she was a schoolgirl?

45 Whose dad slept with his son's granny?

46 Who was Deek's first girlfriend?

47 Eileen married Tommy but then had a fling with who?

48 Which straight man did Scott drunkenly declare love to in The Tall Ship?

49 Who did Jo Rossi have an affair with and fall pregnant with her first child to?

50 Which character met his late wife Michelle on the Clydeside picket lines and fell in love with her pre-2002?

51 Who did Eileen have an affair with which called a halt on her marriage to Tommy?

52 Did Shirley and George ever marry?

53 Liz discovered Archie was planning to fake his suicide and run away with (who?) before he was bonked over the head and tossed off a cliff?

54 Ruth lost the baby she had conceived with Marty and blamed it on the stress of finding out about his affair with who?

55 Name Michael Brodie's wife.

56 Which character's affections moved from Amber Murdoch to Annie Sobacz?

57 Which blonde bombshell barmaid did Charlie lose his virginity to?

58 Hayley ended up having a fling with Jack. But why was this problematic for her family?

59 Iona had an affair with her late sister Shona's ex-husband Tony when she was 16. True or false?

60 After Jimmy endangered the life of baby Madonna by getting involved in another of McCabe's drug deals, what did Scarlett demand?

For answers, please turn to page 102

13

Clydeside Crime

Taggart doesn't have a divine right to the seedier side of Glasgow. There's plenty of dark deeds taking place around Montego Street. Watch your back . . .

1. Who turned out to be the Shieldinch sex attacker?

2. How did Big Bob end up in the clink?

3. Gangster Theresa O'Hara held hairdresser Hayley hostage after Robbie ran up big debts doing what?

4. Which boxing coach battered Lenny in 2009, witnessed by a shocked Malcolm?

5. How is Ewan Murdoch connected to his one-time girlfriend Sammi's ex-squeeze?

6. How did Ewan try to evade arrest for that particular misdemeanor?

7. Which rhyming con-woman tricked Raymond out of his savings?

8. Which Shieldinch bad guy was garrotted after his plan to rob gangster Lenny Murdoch in a jewel heist went wrong?

9. Where was Raymond dumped by the woman who duped him out of his savings?

10 Just when his memory started to return, what was Douglas (Archie) being put on trial for?

11 Who vandalised George Henderson's bench the week after he died?

12 How many times over was Shona a bigamist?

13 Which ranking had Eddie Hunter attained in the police when he was shot?

14 Who did Archie owe money to, giving him cause to try to get his hands on his mother's savings?

15 How did Shellsuit Bob expose Lazy Rays as a brothel?

16 When Marty teamed up with a hooker who was he shocked to discover it was?

17 Who took Romeo and Franco hostage?

18 Who shot gangster JP in Lazy Rays?

19 Which criminal act left Jimmy in a wheelchair?

20 When a hostage situation broke out at 2/1, 5 Montego Street, who was being held there?

**For More Clydeside Crime,
continue directly on to the next quiz.**

For answers, please turn to page 102

15

More Clydeside Crime

And they call Glasgow the Dear Green Place with all this talk of murder and mayhem? Don't have nightmares, do sleep well . . .

21 Who was the man doing the hostage taking at 5 Montego Street?

22 Which unlikely OAP hero saved the day?

23 What landmark episode did this Montego Street siege mark? a) 100 b) 200 c) 500

24 Which unlikely figure showed compassion by bribing the prison guards to take Stevie to a warehouse for a family reunion when he was being transferred from jail to jail?

25 Why did Shellsuit Bob go through a phase of stashing drugs in his garage?

26 Gilbert Martin played released convict Paddy Adams in 2003. What prison had he spent time in?

27 Who were the Shieldinch rapist's three victims before he was killed?

28 The terror girl-gang left a dead rat as part of a bullying campaign against which pensioner?

29 John Morrison played dodgy criminal defence lawyer McKenna – but who hired him to get her off with the murder of Dr McKenzie?

30 Heather walked free from court after standing trial for the murder of Marcus McKenzie. But who was stabbed outside the court after the verdict?

31 Who lied in court to get Heather off the hook?

32 Hazel set off to visit her dad in Inverness, but before she could get there what did stepbrother Brian do?

33 When baby Franco was abducted who found him in the back seat of a 4WD in 2002?

34 Which cantankerous old taxi driver racially abused Zara Malik?

35 Which former jailbird returned to Shieldinch from prison in the first episode?

36 Malcolm was very nearly caught up in a fire at the doocot but which troublesome teen set the fire?

37 Who rescued Hazel from her kidnapping at the hands of Brian?

38 Marcus McKenzie's daughter turned up and avenged her father's killing by stabbing who outside the court?

39 Mac was run out of town by the Hendersons – but only because he'd turned his attentions on which young lady?

40 When Nicki found Marty in bed with her prostitute sister, how did he try to get her to keep schtum?

For answers, please turn to page 103

Siblings in the City

From Jo and Ruth to the mixed up Murdochs, the sibling rivalry on the river has been a constant source of storylines for the soap's scriptwriters. But how many have left a lasting impression on you?

1. Arrange Shona, Iona and Roisin in order of age starting with the eldest.

2. Arrange Scarlett's brood in order of age, youngest to oldest.

3. Which of Roisin's sisters had an affair with Marty Green?

4. Name the three Brodie Brothers.

5. Arrange them in age oldest to youngest.

6. Name Michael's kids.

7. Which Shieldinch siblings went head to head over Sonny's plans to open a fast food outlet at the Conway Spices site?

8. What were Tina and Eddie's sons called?

9. Which flame haired hussy has slept with her sister's husband and also her pal Roisin's?

10. Name George Henderson's brother who turned up and caused mayhem in his home.

19

11 Which bisexual ex-soldier postman went to jail for selling drugs out the back of his mum's icey when his sister grassed him up?

12 Which of the Rossi sisters did Cormac cheat on the other with?

13 Which character is both a great-granda and an original cast member?

14 Shabana Akhtar Bakhsh played which of the Malik sisters?

15 What was Luca's relationship to Jo Rossi in the end? a) brother b) stepbrother c) half brother d) none of the above

16 Who's the big sister out of Eileen and Gina?

17 Do they have any other siblings?

18 Eileen slept with a man she eventually became the accomplice in the attempted murder of. Who?

19 Are Jo and Ruth Rossi full or half sisters?

20 Which of the Brodie brothers broke in to the Shieldinch medical surgery to get drugs to support his prescription drug habit?

For answers, please turn to page 103

Soapy Doubles

It's been 'the Scottish soap' since it started, with poor old *High Road* biting the dust soon after. But many of the *River City* regulars have popped up in other soap operas on telly. Have you spotted them?

1 Who is the only member of the soap's cast to have had both a starring role in *River City* and also *Neighbours*?

2 Which *River City* star played Calum McNeill in the Gaelic soap *Machair*?

3 Who played a medic on *EastEnders* treating Nick Cotton a year before joining *River City* as an original cast member? a) John Murtagh, b) Mamta Kash c) Libby McArthur

4 Which original and long serving member of the *River City* cast played Andy Cameron's character's wife on STV soap *Take The High Road*?

5 Which Saturday night TV programme was the actress who played Hana Malik previously associated with? a) *The National Lottery Draw* b) *Cagney & Lacey* c) *Casualty*

6 When *River City* ran its *Indecent Proposal* style storyline in 2003, which other British soap also explored similar territory in the same year?

7 Gilly Gilchrist played a Casanova chef by the name of Billy Taylor in which other British soap?

8 Which Irish actress, who shares her name with the lead singer of Travis, also starred in Irish soap *Fair City*?

9 Jacqueline Leonard played Lydia Murdoch in *River City*, but who did she play in *EastEnders*?

10 Who popped up in *Hollyoaks* as mystery woman Caroline Cooper after her spell as Kirsty Henderson in *River City*?

11 Which former *River City* star was at the centre of an Old Firm stooshie when his Celtic-supporting character in *Coronation Street* received complaints from Rangers fans, prompting *Corrie* bosses to alter his scripts?

12 Louise Jamieson played vivacious Viv in *River City*. But who did she play in *EastEnders*?

13 What do *River City* lads Sam Robertson and Iain de Caestecker have in common?

14 Sheila Grier turned up in *River City* as Charlie Bowie's mum in 2009. Which Scouse soap was she in 25 years earlier as Sandra Maghie?

15 Which blonde bombshell cast member turned up as a preoperative transsexual called Steve in BBC1 daytime soap *Doctors* in 2011?

16 Ewan Murdoch and Bradley Branning in *EastEnders* both met similar fates in 2010. What were they?

17 Who is the only actor to have appeared in a soap north and south of the border at the same time?

18 *River City* was the Scottish soap he appeared in, but what was the other one he was in at the same time?

19 Which former *EastEnders* actor (hint: he played Sanjay Kapoor in the Walford soap) signed on at Shieldinch to play a gay undertaker who was run out of town after a brief fling with Scott?

20 Eileen McCallum achieved fame in which STV soap before playing Liz Buchanan in *River City*?

For answers, please turn to page 104

Family Ties

They're the lynchpins of the community – or the bane of the back courts. Without the families of Shieldinch, things would be a lot quieter down Montego Street. How well do you know them?

Clan Murdoch

1 Lee wasn't Lydia's real son – who hired him to pose as the kid she gave away for adoption?

2 Who took Lenny hostage in the bungled jewel heist?

3 What did Ewan and Lenny have stashed in a warehouse, which led to Amber being rushed to hospital?

4 Ewan was an ex a) fighter pilot b) marine c) TA officer.

5 Who did Lenny hold hostage at the riverside?

6 Which two characters plunged into the Clyde together after this siege?

7 When Lenny pulled a gun on McCabe, who ran into Bob's garage and knocked it out of his hand?

8 Which Holy man whacked Lenny over the head with a giant spanner in Bob's garage after he'd had a stand off with a gun and McCabe?

9 Amber, Fraser and Jimmy were involved in an elaborate sting to put McCabe down in 2011. But which criminal played a pivotal part in the plan?

10 Name Lydia and Lenny's only child together.

11 Who is Rory Murdoch's dad?

12 Lydia & Lenny's only child together was the product of an affair between the pair when Lenny was still married to Mary. True or false?

13 Who locked Amber in a cupboard and planted the keys in her mate Jen's bag?

14 Who turned out to be the stranger lurking in the car after Fraser's botched affair with the McCabe drug deal?

15 When Lenny Murdoch first showed up in Shieldinch, how many of his family did he have in tow?

16 Amber's accent is Scottish. Rory's accent is Scottish. Lydia's accent lies somewhere in between Surrey and Shetland. Lenny's accent is Scottish. Ewan Murdoch's accent is . . . ?

17 Hola is a) a Spanish tapas bar b) a wine merchants c) a clothing boutique.

18 At the start of 2011, Amber Murdoch was the only remnant of the infamous family in the soap. True or false?

19 Lenny made his 2011 return in what kind of car?

20 When Amber called a number she'd been left if she ever got into trouble, she asked for . . . who, without realising it was a code name to get her dad back on the scene? a) Hamish b) Fergus c) Declan?

For answers, please turn to page 104

Family Ties

Clan Rossi

1. Who is eldest sibling out of Jo and Ruth Rossi?

2. What is Romeo Rossi's relationship to Malcolm Hamilton?

3. How did everyone find out about Gina's affair with Jack?

4. Which one of the Rossi sisters did Leo try it on with – despite his brother Gabriel getting there first?

5. What was the name of Ruth's childhood sweetheart who turned up out of the blue?

6. Which character was wrongly accused of giving her young daughter prescription drugs in a storyline which pre-empted her departure from the series?

7. Where did Ruth move to when she left Shieldinch?

8. Ruth dated Harry the cop. True or false?

9. Where did Ruth's runaway husband Andy run away to?

10. At what off-set location did Morag Calder film her character Ruth's departure scenes?

11 What's the name of Ruth's baby?

12 With Ruth suffering from post natal depression, which of her best pals put their foot down to protest over Eilidh being taken to be Christened by her granny Gina?

13 In which country did Marty and Ruth get married?

14 How did Ruth let her hubby Marty know she knew about his secret STD?

15 Who told Marty that Ruth was pregnant to him?

16 Which kid played young Franco when Jo returned to the series (with a different head)?

17 Where had she been?

18 Who has been jailed twice, run over at her mother's wedding, left in a coma, and had her son kidnapped and tragically killed after a car crash?

19 Who had a baby to Nazir, then bedded her sister's latest squeeze soon after?

20 What's Gina and Eileen's maiden name?

For answers, please turn to page 104

Family Ties

The Adams Family

1 What's Scarlett's nickname for Shellsuit Bob?

2 Kelly Marie left Shieldinch to move abroad with her footballer boyfriend Andrew. But where did they go?

3 Father Michael became embroiled in a messy tug of love with two women after his affections. Kelly Marie was one of them. Who was the other one?

4 Which member of her brood did Scarlett keep secret the fact that she wasn't their real mother?

5 Name Scarlett and Big Bob's mum.

6 Who arrived in Shieldinch first? Big Bob or Molly?

7 Who made a Christmas appearance as a runaway Santa escaping from his job in a department store to Shieldinch?

8 What did Scarlett spot on Professor Michael Learmonth that made her suspect he could be the Shieldinch sex attacker?

9 What's Theresa's relationship to Scarlett?

10 Before arriving at Shieldinch, in which establishment had Scarlett's sister Theresa been residing?

11 What's Madonna's relationship to Stevie and Kelly Marie?

12 After Theresa showed up in Shieldinch with shocking revelations, Bob was no longer brother or stepbrother to Kelly Marie, Stevie or Madonna. So what was he?

13 Nicki left Bob, packing her bags and heading for Spain after he committed which textbook error?

14 In which highland town did Tattie and Big Bob meet?

15 What's Scarlett's maiden name?

16 An Irish professor caused upset in which household when his poetry lessons ignited a spark between teacher and pupil?

17 Who was revived from a coma by an ice cream van?

18 Name Jimmy's beloved rescue dog.

19 Who went under cover to expose Lazy Rays as a brothel?

20 How could Scarlett, Jimmy and the gang afford a posh Christmas lunch in a swanky hotel?

21 Who had a brief addiction to internet gambling?

22 Scarlett and Jimmy live at 9 Montego Street but on which floor?

23 How did Jimmy end up in a wheelchair?

24 Why couldn't Scarlett cook the turkey at Christmas in 2004?

25 What's Paddy Adams' relationship to Kelly Marie and Stevie?

For answers, please turn to page 105

Arrivals & Departures

There have been a lot of comings and goings since cameras started rolling down by the river in 2002. How many ins and outs do you recall?

1 Where had Lily returned to Shieldinch from when she arrived?

2 Who made her Shieldinch debut in the back of her dad's taxi?

3 What was her birthday?

4 How did Sonny make his entrance?

5 The first words in the debut episode in 2002 were uttered by who?

6 And what were those first words? a) 'Hullawrerrchina.' b) 'Fandabbydozy.' c) 'The wedding's aff.'

7 Which character, when being trailed for his debut in Shieldinch by the BBC publicity ads, walked down the street to the sound of The Verve track 'Lucky Man'?

8 Which character came into the soap as a leader of a girl gang who was blackmailing Dr Shah into giving her drugs to sell?

9 Who made his entrance with a short-lived goatee beard dressed all in black and in a black Mercedes?

10 Which recovering alcoholic made her return to Shieldinch and her character's debut in a Hogmanay episode 2002?

11 The viewing figures for the first episode were a) 810,000 b) 400,000 c) 220,000.

12 What shock awaited Tommy Donachie and wife Eileen when they returned from Honeymoon in the second episode?

13 What was the reason for Marty's 2008 return?

14 Marty stole his kid off Ruth and tried to escape across – what?

15 Which character – whose namesake is Scotland's best ever tennis player – took his lady to Monaco to live?

16 Where did Tony Kearney film their final scenes?

17 Where did he move to?

18 When Ruth and Scott left there were only six original cast members left. Name them.

19 What was the storyline around Zoe leaving Shieldinch?

20 Gray O'Brien was in *Corrie* and *River City* at the same time but when Billy Davies said he was leaving where was he bound?

21 What country did Jo go to when she ran off with Luca?

22 Who tried to kill himself in a stolen car but ended up killing his granny instead?

23 Where had Alice Henderson originally run off to when she abandoned her son?

24 When she finally left Shieldinch, was it by subway or taxi?

25 Bisexual bad boy Stevie left Shieldinch for the jail after selling drugs out the back of the icey – but who grassed him up?

For answers, please turn to page 105

Montego Street Marriages

They say the path of true love never runs smooth – and you could say the same thing about most of the weddings that have taken place down *River City* way. Memorable for all the wrong reasons . . .

1 Who was run over by a taxi on the day of her mum's wedding?

2 Who was driving the taxi?

3 What did Lorraine Kelly do at Gina's wedding?

4 When she married Raymond on her deathbed, bigamist Shona was marrying him for what time?

5 Where did Ruth and Marty get married?

6 How did Gina discover Douglas was a really cynical cover up for Archie – and that Liz knew old Archie was back before she did?

7 What was the reason given for Kelly Marie's absence at her mum's wedding to Jimmy?

8 Charlie and Bob were all set to get married at a double wedding with Scarlett and Jimmy. Who called it off, him or her?

9 Where did Vader and Hazel get married?

10 What happened to Jimmy and Bob on their joint stag night?

11 Who did Scarlett ask to be her matron of honour at her marriage to Jimmy?

12 Which of Shona's husbands turned up desperate to win her back as she proposed to Raymond?

13 What was the tune played at Raymond and Roisin's wedding? a) 'Run' by Snow Patrol b) 'Help' by The Beatles c) 'Sunshine on Leith' by The Proclaimers.

14 Name the church on Montego Street where the *River City* weddings take place.

15 What did Gina and her daughters sing at the karaoke at Tommy and Eileen's wedding? a) 'Every Breath You Take' by The Police b) 'My Favourite Mistake' by Sheryl Crow c) 'Young Hearts Run Free' by Candi Staton

16 Gina snogged which toyboy at her sister's wedding reception?

17 The Rossi girls, Ruth, Gina and Jo clubbed together to get newlyweds Tommy and Eileen a weekend away to where as their wedding present in episode one? a) Loch Fyne b) London c) Liverpool

18 What theme of wedding did Raymond and Roisin have?

19 Who was in charge of the video camera on the fateful day of Jimmy and Scarlett's wedding – starting the ball rolling on the storyline where Gina found out Archie was back?

20 Hazel and Vader said until death do us part . . . but name the girl who came along and changed all that.

For answers, please turn to page 106

Christmas on Clydeside

'Tis the season to be jolly.' Or at least have a laugh at the fantastically far-fetched festive storylines scriptwriters gift us with come 25 December. No peeking . . .

1. Who drugged Liz on Christmas Day?

2. How did a Christmas surprise for baby Madonna go into meltdown in the Mullen household?

3. Scarlett gave birth to Madonna in a) The Tall Ship b) the living room floor c) a taxi.

4. What was playing on the radio when she gave birth to Madonna? a) 'Baby I Love You' b) 'Real Gone Kid' c) 'When You Wish Upon a Star'

5. When Eileen had baby Stewart, where did her waters break?

6. Who was given a special *It's a Wonderful Life* style storyline in a festive special in 2008?

7. Who played his Guardian Angel?

8. What did Eileen not want anyone else to do at Christmas dinner before she went into labour?

9 Who collapsed with a cancer diagnosis in the Christmas episode of 2010?

10 Which patriarchal figure died on Christmas Day surrounded by his family including a daughter that wasn't his?

For answers, please turn to page 107

They say Scotland is the sick man of Europe, which must make Shieldinch the fur on the nation's arteries. From paralysis to alcoholism the NHS budget for Montego Street could run a small country. The doctor will see you now . . .

1 Whose dizzy turns led to a diagnosis of epilepsy?

2 Which old Clydesider revealed he was suffering from mesothelioma in 2010?

3 Where did Malcolm decide to book tickets for after the medical news? a) Australia b) Rothesay c) The Pavilion Panto

4 How did Molly find out Scarlett had cancer?

5 Who was wrongly accused of giving her daughter prescription drugs?

6 Soldier Liam Brodie was addicted to painkillers. True or false?

7 How did Bob end up in a coma?

8 What happened to Gerry after his cocaine addiction got out of hand?

9   And where was his character dispatched to after Heather decided she couldn't cope with looking after him?

10 Who told her boyfriend she knew about his secret sex scandal by putting a leaflet about STDs in his Valentine's Day card?

11 Which *River City* kid was admitted to hospital with alcohol poisoning and why?

12 How did Roisin end up in a coma?

13 Who took over from Vinnie Shah in the Shieldinch surgery after he committed suicide?

14 Who attacked Gina and left her in a coma?

15 Which character had an incontinent episode after a bevvy session?

16 Who had a termination after finding out her unborn baby would die in the womb?

17 Who gave Malcolm a biscuit with a 'secret herb' to help with his arthritis?

18 And what was the secret herb?

19 Which character seemed to be developing dementia in the second year of the soap but went on for another eight years at least without any memory degeneration?

20 Which character secretly started filming Hazel during his cannabis psychosis?

**For More Medical Matters,
continue directly on to the next quiz.**

For answers, please turn to page 107

More Medical Matters

Maybe it's the lack of sunshine or bad diet. Or probably just the fact that there's not a lot of drama when soap opera characters are healthy all the time . . .

21 Who was injected by a contaminated syringe?

22 What was the syringe contaminated with?

23 Ruth suffered from a mental health problem eventually diagnosed as borderline personality disorder. True or false?

24 Which now robust and reformed young character and budding radio disk-jockey started drinking aged just 11 to help her cope with a chaotic life in and out of care homes?

25 Ruth took the blame for giving a flu jab to a patient who shouldn't have been given it. When the patient fell ill from the injection Ruth was suspended temporarily by Michael. But who 'fessed up' to hiding a note about the patient?

26 After Alice Henderson was killed off, which of her relatives hit the bottle to cope?

27 Which character opted to disguise his follicular degeneration by briefly wearing a wig?

28 Which key character successfully battled ovarian cancer?

29 Who was Alice Henderson's alcoholism sponsor in the community?

30 George Henderson died surrounded by his family – but what killed him?

For answers, please turn to page 107

You Can Choose Your Friends, But Not Your Family

It's not just about the Rossis, the Murdochs and the Adams, you know. How closely have you been following the domestic dramas behind the other doors?

1. How many years had the soap been running before Shellsuit Bob found out Scarlett wasn't his real mum?

2. Name the character Lydia thought was her long lost son who she'd given up for adoption.

3. What's the relationship between Shellsuit Bob and Big Bob?

4. Which member of Hayley's family turned up out of the blue seeking a shoulder to cry on?

5. Scott's dad John arrived in Shieldinch needing a kidney transplant that Scott offered to be the donor for. But why did John refuse?

6. Which former jailbird turned up in town to rock Shellsuit Bob's world with some stunning news about his birth?

7. What's Theresa's relationship to Scarlett?

8. What's Madonna's relationship to Kelly Marie and Stevie Adams?

9. What's Madonna's relationship to Shellsuit Bob?

10 Who is Fraser's dad?

11 Who played George's brother Robert?

12 How did Archie try to kill his mum Liz?

13 Why did Alice Henderson cause a scene at George's funeral?

14 Who was her dad?

15 Who packed Alice Henderson's bags for her and chucked her out into the street?

16 After his behaviour went off the rails, Paul Hunter was packed off to a new school. Where?

17 Why did Liz take an overdose?

18 Which two characters actually pushed Archie off the cliff?

19 Who hit Archie over the head as he tried to strangle his wife Gina?

20 What did she use to strike him?

For a continuation of Relative Values, proceed directly on to the next quiz.

For answers, please turn to page 107

Relative Values

The Shieldinch family saga continues . . .

21 What relation to Nicole Brodie is Leyla Brodie?

22 What's the name of Michael Brodie's teenage son?

23 What's Deek's relation to Raymond?

24 Deek and Brian Henderson were cousins. How?

25 Who is Bob Adam's stepdad?

26 Adeeb Brodie expressed an interest to his parents to learn more about the culture of his homeland. But where's his family from?

27 When Shona married Raymond, what did her relationship to Shirley become?

28 On the verge of becoming foster parents, Eileen and Raymond found out – what?

29 If Theresa is Bob's mum, who is his dad?

30 Which member of Scarlett's brood turned out to fancy men and women?

For answers, please turn to page 108

Guest Appearances

Among the Shieldinch regulars, there have been one or two other familiar faces popping up in the City. Who did you spot?

1. Which breakfast TV host turned up at Gina's wedding?

2. What part did Glasgow Warriors rugby player Gary Dempsey play during his Shieldinch cameo?

3. Which then Kilmarnock FC player made a brief cameo in the soap in 2010?

4. Which famous Rab C Nesbitt star appeared as a gardener who was a witness at Shona and Raymond's wedding?

5. When the Adams headed off to a posh hotel for a Christmas day treat, which famous Scottish actress played the vexed hotel boss who had to deal with them?

6. Which bizarre Scottish TV funny man had a brief cameo role when he walked through a shot featuring Malcolm Hamilton?

7. Which Radio One DJ landed a part in the soap after he initiated a campaign to have the show broadcast across the UK?

8 Which *Chewin' The Fat* character made a cameo on *River City* as part of a comedy sketch for the Hogmanay comedy show?

9 Billy Connolly made a brief guest appearance at Jimmy's stag do. True or false?

10 Lorraine Kelly played herself, but who was her 'character' supposed to be a pal of? a) Billy Davies b) Hana Malik c) Liz Hamilton

For answers, please turn to page 108

Life Beyond Shieldinch

While every soap needs its mainstays, nothing is forever, especially not if you're an actor. Many of your Shieldinch favourites have had some interesting careers before and after *River City*. Have you been paying attention?

1. Which actor who played a priest in Shieldinch appeared in *Batman Begins*?

2. Which Tiree-raised *RC* star was in *Dramarama* with *Dr Who* star David Tennant in his acting youth?

3. *Colin & Cumberland* was an animated mini-series that helped non-Gaelic speakers speak Gaelic. Which *RC* cast member voiced it?

4. Tom Urie is one of the soap's most popular characters, but which BBC Scotland show did he appear in as one half of the cabaret duo Almost Angelic?

5. Which two former *RC* blokes turned up in Channel 4 youth drama *Skins*?

6. Which former *Taggart* star featured as politician Nick Morrison?

7. Which former *River City* teen played young journalist Paddy Meehan in BBC1's thriller *The Field of Blood*?

8 Name the hedonistic BBC Scotland drama in which David Paisley starred in a decade before he turned up in *River City*.

9 Which former *River City* starlet appeared in BBC Scotland hospital drama *Zig Zag Love* opposite Bobby Carlyle and Joe McFadden?

10 Who played Ashley Jensen's mum in the hilarious BBC Scotland Rabbie Burns comedy *No Holds Bard*?

11 Which member of the Shieldinch cast played first officer William Murdoch in the blockbuster movie *Titanic*?

12 Which Shieldinch stalwart went head to head with Jackie Bird's BBC Scotland Hogmanay coverage presenting BBC Alba's first ever live Hogmanay hootenanny from Stornoway?

13 Which member of the *RC* cast popped up in STV drama *Cracked* as a salesman suffering from the mental health disorder hypo-mania?

14 Kieron Elliott went from *River City* to which US bloodsucking vampire drama?

15 Name the Jersey-based detective series in which Louise Jamieson shot to fame in the 1980s.

16 Who did Louise Jamieson play in *Dr Who*? a) Martha b) Leela c) K-9

17 Who starred in *Dream Team* on Sky before making a transfer to *River City*?

18 Who plays a recurring character in Sanjeev Kohli's comedy *Fags, Bags and Mags* on Radio 4?

19 Cora Bisset played a bitchy ex-jailbird called Yvonne, but she also starred in which Glasgow-based tower block drama on a rival Scottish channel?

20 Which *RC* actor has also starred in *Rome* and *Low Winter Sun* as well as internationally award-winning Canadian drama *Durham County*?

For answers, please turn to page 108

Ship Shape

It's the central focus of any soap opera – the local boozer. The Tall Ship is over 100 years old. But this pub quiz will only take you back over the last decade. How much do you remember through the alcohol haze?

1 Which crimper caused surprise when he blurted out the news that he was Hayley's father in The Tall Ship?

2 Who had to dress up as an olive for a promotional day at The Tall Ship?

3 Which of the following characters has never done a shift at the Ship? a) Scott Wallace b) Ewan Murdoch c) Scarlett Mullen d) Liz Buchanan

4 Lenny Murdoch was once owner of The Tall Ship. True or false?

5 When Raymond took a 'break' from running The Tall Ship, which couple did he happily hand the keys over to?

6 What was the name of the restaurant in The Tall Ship?

7 What did Hazel say in front of a crowded bar in the hope that Vader wouldn't dump her for Alanna?

8 How many chimney pots are there on the two chimney-stacks atop The Tall Ship? a) six b) eight c) twelve

9 What colour is the door to The Tall Ship?

10 How many windows are there on the ground floor to the front of The Tall Ship? a) two b) four c) six

54

Parenthood

They say a child is a reflection on its parents – and that doesn't say much for the maws and paws of Shieldinch. But with role models like these, what else would you expect?

1 Teen tearaway Alanna turned up as the long lost daughter of which big-expressioned character?

2 Who did Della fall pregnant to – Billy Davies or Lewis Cope?

3 Why could Billy and Della not have kids together?

4 Which original character discovered he was the product of his mum's affair with her old schoolteacher?

5 Who slept with both Alice and her mum (but not at the same time!)?

6 Who is Della's mum?

7 Who fathered a baby after a one-night stand *Indecent Proposal* style?

8 Who bought a baby from gymslip mum Michelle?

9 Rochelle was the baby involved in the buy-a-baby storyline, but what was her name changed to?

10 Junkie Patricia Cullen was the mother of which pair of sisters?

11 What age was Alice Henderson when she gave birth to Deek?

12 Who's Gina's Dad?

13 Who is Jo and Ruth's Granda?

14 Jo Cameron Brown played Moira – who was her son?

15 Who is Ewan's mum?

16 Lenny is Ewan's dad. True or false?

17 Amber is Ewan and Lydia's daughter. True or false.

18 What was Lydia's relationship to Rory?

19 How many children did Karim and Hana Malik have?

20 When Jo gave birth to Romeo, her other half Billy had no idea that (who?) was the real father?

For answers, please turn to page 109

A Shieldinch Stroll

It's one of the most impressive purpose-built TV sets in Europe, according to experts. At £10 million, you'd expect it to be. So let's enjoy a dander around Scotland's most famous fictional street . . .

1 What did Heavenly Herbals spring up in place of?

2 Who ran Heavenly Herbals?

3 When Gordon Swan bought Moda Vida from Shirley what did he change its name to?

4 Which original character waited five years before he was given a home that was represented on-screen?

5 What was the Hunters' address? a) 20 Montego Street b) 20 Shieldinch Way c) 20 Ship Street

6 What was the address of Lydia's boutique? a) 22 All Saints Road b) 22 Matalan Way c) 22 Montego Street

7 What was Hola before it was a boutique? a) Chinese take away b) flower shop c) Oxfam

8 Who lives up the stairs behind the old Victorian washhouse?

9 What number of Montego Street did Ruth and Marty live at? a) 5 b) 55 c) 205

10 Who lived in what became known as 'the young persons' flat' originally?

11. Which two shops were knocked together to make the new look hair salon Number 18?

12. On what location was there a proposed drive-through burger joint?

13. When the series started, which family lived above the grocer's shop?

14. Where's the bus stop? a) opposite the Oyster Café b) opposite The Tall Ship c) at the boat yard

15. Is there a fountain or a bandstand across the street from The Tall Ship?

16. There's no post box in Shieldinch. True or false?

17. Is there a phone box?

18. We've never seen a subway train arriving in Shieldinch. True or false?

19. What colour is the paintwork on the fountain?

20. What colour is the lettering on the sign above the door of The Tall Ship?

**For More Around Montego,
continue directly on to the next quiz.**

For answers, please turn to page 109

Sit down and take a quick breather on George's bench. The second part of the *River City* tour is about to begin . . .

21 In the opening credits, punters can be seen walking across a bridge on the River Clyde. Which one?

22 What connects *River City* to a water-based Glasgow tourist attraction known as Glenlee?

23 How many booths are there in the Oyster Café? a) three b) four c) five

24 What words are on the signage above the Ship door? a) choice malts and fine ales b) cheap booze and loose women c) hard men and sore faces

25 What's the name of the local newspaper in Shieldinch? a) Clyde Enquirer b) Shieldinch Slip c) Daily River

26 There's a sign for a mode of transport discreetly placed around the streets of Shieldinch. Is it a) ferry b) hovercraft c) seaplane?

27 Which pub was the inspiration for The Tall Ship? a) The Ferry Inn, Renfrew b) The Louden Tavern, Glasgow c) Bairds Bar, Glasgow

28 Which Shieldinch meeting place is at 12 Montego Street?

29 There's a quiet lane leading from Montego Street to the Cycle Path and ferry terminal. Is it called a) Paton's Lane b) Alanna's Alley c) Robert's Road?

30 The Pend is which part of Shieldinch famed for sneaky kisses?

31 What does it say in the window of the Oyster Café? a) cigarettes and ices b) chocs and ginger c) coffee and donuts

32 Which item of outsized confectionary sits outside the Oyster Café?

33 What recreation ground lies behind Hola and Number 18?

34 What colour is the lettering on the sign for the Oyster Café?

35 Which OAP moved into a flat shared by Bob and Deek?

36 Where did Malcolm declare love for Liz?

37 Which of Ruth's runaway husbands ran from the streets of Shieldinch to . . . Dubai?

38 Name Scott's boyfriend who took him from the streets of River City to the Lake District after nine years.

39 There's an old traditional Victorian washhouse in Shieldinch – where is it?

40 According to the *River City* history annals, in the 1800s, sailors would come by and spend time with ladies of the night upstairs from which establishment?

For answers, please turn to page 110

Moving on to a Better Place

The only certainties in life are death and taxes (and rain in Shieldinch for most of the summer). Many of the soap's favourite faces have passed over to the other side. How well do you remember them?

1. Which two key people in Jo Rossi's life died together in a car accident?

2. What do the characters Alice Henderson, Kirsty Henderson, Franco Rossi and Nazir Malik all have in common?

3. Why did Jo and Gina hold Ruth responsible for the death of Franco and Nazir?

4. How did Jimmy's dog Alfie die?

5. Which two bodies were found buried in the Shieldinch boatyard?

6. Who finally killed Archie?

7. Who lay dead in a flat next door to the students for days in 2010?

8. How did Alice Henderson die?

9. Moira Henderson died after a car crash – but who was at the wheel of the car?

10 How did Shona McIntyre die?

11 What was her dying wish for deathbed hubby Raymond?

12 Where did they bury Shona?

13 Which character was so haunted by running someone over that he started seeing apparitions of him?

14 How did George Henderson die?

15 Who killed DCI Eddie Hunter?

16 Which Shieldinch bad guy was garroted by a surprise passenger when he got into the front seat of a car?

17 Who killed Sammy the Snitch and how?

18 What happened to end Kirsty Henderson's life?

19 How did lesbian lawyer Fi die?

20 Which member of the Murdoch clan tried to contact Eddie Hunter with a Ouija board?

For more Dispatches on the Banks of the Clyde, continue directly on to the next quiz.

For answers, please turn to page 110

Dispatches on the Banks of the Clyde

Well, come on. Does Shieldinch look to you like the kind of place to buck a nation's dismal death statistics? Look closely at this lot and you might be able to figure out which number of Montego Street the Grim Reaper actually lives at . . .

21 How did Alanna's dad Alex die?

22 Who found Dr Marcus McKenzie knifed to death in his office?

23 Who had knifed him?

24 Who was the first *River City* character to be murdered?

25 Tommy was killed by the Shieldinch strangler but not by strangulation. How did he kill him?

26 Who had to formally identify Alice Henderson's body after she was killed in a car accident?

27 Did Lorraine McIntosh's character return to be killed off?

28 When Archie was disposed of over the cliff, what was the tell-tale sign given to viewers that he could still be alive – that Eileen and Gina hadn't been privy to?

29 Name the odd one out from these Shieldinch departers: George Henderson, Alice Henderson, Moira Henderson, Brian Henderson.

30 George Henderson came back and haunted the clients of the Shieldinch community centre at their Christmas dinner. True or false?

For answers, please turn to page 111

Working Nine to Five

Economic downturn? What economic downturn? In Shieldinch, there's been a surprising amount of work around. Butcher, baker, candlestick maker . . . actually, no, none of them here. But plenty else besides . . .

1 Who took work as a pest control officer against his wife's wishes?

2 Innes Maitland was a) an arts student b) a chemistry student c) a medical student.

3 What was Daniel McKee's wife Marianne's profession?

4 Where did Carly quit working to open Carly's Cafe?

5 Which drug addict's daughter got work alongside Bob in the garage?

6 Russell Barr played camp incomer and fitness instructor Jake Munro. But what did he also teach?

7 Who originally ran Hola?

8 What was the name of Marty's business that he ran from a dingy Portakabin?

9 Buchanan Associates was a) a lawyer's firm, b) a coal merchants or c) an estate agents.

10 Who were the named partners at McGrade and Kydd Solicitors?

11 The Tall Ship Grill eaterie eventually made way for a pool room. True or false.

12 Texas cowboy Sonny Munro rode into town in 2007 and threatened to open a) a fast food joint, b) a petrol station or c) a charity shop?

13 What was Shellsuit Bob's fiancée Charlie Drummond's job?

14 Where did Carly's mum Lola work?

15 Which matriarchal figure had a 50% stake in Moda Vida?

16 What profession was Kelly Marie's boyfriend before she started snogging priests?

17 Which team did Andrew play for?

18 What was Deek's coffee café called?

19 Which budding entrepreneur tried his hand at window cleaning before settling on something more mechanical?

20 What was Heather Bellshaw's profession when she arrived in Shieldinch?

For more on Shieldinch Industries Ltd, continue directly on to the next quiz.

For answers, please turn to page 111

Shieldinch Industries Ltd

For a small place with one street running through it, there really is an awful lot of work going around . . .

21 Heather Bellshaw went on to run which bar?

22 When he wasn't working on the icey with his maw, what was Stevie's main job around Shieldinch?

23 What was Della's job?

24 Who turned the trendy hair salon into a haven for the blue rinse brigade when Della and Billy went on holiday?

25 Which character's child abuse was seen as a reason for her teenage rebellion and eventual stint as a lap dancer?

26 Who was the senior partner at Buchanan Associates?

27 Scott Wallace was originally a) a graphic designer b) a newspaper sub editor c) a magazine writer

28 Who was a receptionist in Lazy Rays?

29 What was George Henderson's job?

30 Name the guy in the Oyster Café who serves coffee but rarely speaks.

31 Who chucked a university course to open a print business in Shieldinch?

32 What was the resulting print shop called?

33 Who did Tommy Donachie inherit The Tall Ship from?

34 Who launched The Base to help support the youth of Shieldinch?

35 What happened to spell the end of Versus?

36 Who did Deek sell Deekafe to?

37 Which character dropped out of Uni and struggled for ages to keep it a secret from everyone but his best mate Innes?

38 Which widower landed the job of community centre manager?

39 Who opened an arcade in Shieldinch?

40 Which of Malcolm's daughters got involved in local politics?

For answers, please turn to page 111

Behind the Scenes at Shieldinch

Don't look behind the curtain or you'll ruin the magic . . .
Och, maybe just a quick peek then . . .

1. John Rooney joined *River City* as a writer after rave reviews for his other Glasgow-set domestic drama on STV. Name that drama.

2. David McKay was a director on *River City* but he was also an actor who appeared in *My Name is Joe* and *Braveheart*. Name the 80s kids drama he was the star of.

3. What major – and unpopular – change took place in the way *River City* was broadcast in October 2008?

4. Which leading star of teaching drama *Waterloo Road* ended up working behind the camera on *River City* as a director?

5. Jason Merrells made one very brief appearance in front of cameras when directing *River City*. But it wasn't in person. How did it happen?

6. What doubles for ice cream in the Oyster Café? a) cream cheese b) butter c) mozzarella

7. Which Scottish singing star once claimed she had come up with the idea for *River City*, but had the allegation categorically refuted by the BBC?

8 Who created *River City*?

9 Which patriarchal taxi driving character briefly had his BBC publicity photograph accidentally (mischievously?) replaced by his namesake the hippo from *Rainbow* in publicity material?

10 In 2007 which London-born Scotland-loving mega-star singer was unsuccessfully approached with a view to taking a guest star part in the soap?

11 How did actor Gilly Gilchrist reach the position where Archie was washed up on the beach in Berwickshire? a) parachute b) zip slide c) abseil

12 What do they use to represent coffee on *River City*? a) Bovril b) cola c) coffee

13 They look like sandstone but what are the tenements made from? a) papier mache and sand b) wood and CGI editing c) concrete and plaster

14 Are the flowers in the ground at *River City*? a) real b) wooden c) plastic

15 The beer in The Tall Ship is real beer. True or false?

16 Many of the cast talk about 'double banking' when they speak of the filming process. What is that?

17 What significant event in the history of how *River City* was broadcast happened one Sunday in June 2003?

18 Who is the *River City* theme tunes' original composer?
a) John Williams b) Lorne Balfe c) Rachmaninov

19 *River City* creator Stephen Greenhorn also wrote which hit musical based on the songs of which Scottish band?

20 What was the site of the *River City* set formerly used as?
a) J&B whisky bottling plant b) Irn Bru factory c) Tunnock's Tea Cakes depot

For more on Making Montego Street, continue directly on to the next quiz.

For answers, please turn to page 112

72

Making Montego Street

What's that? You want MORE of the magic that makes Montego Street come to life? Come right this way . . .

21 Within three months of starting the show's viewing figures had fallen from 810,000 to a) 194,000 b) 200,000 c) 10,000.

22 Shieldinch is located in the Scottish town of a) Dumbarton, b) Dunblane or c) Dalmellington.

23 The cakes and buns in the café and the deli are allegedly covered with what to stop staff eating them?

24 What's the connection between *River City* and dramas *Garrow's Law*, *The Deep*, *Hope Springs* and *God on Trial*?

25 How much BBC money was reportedly allocated to set up *River City*? a) £10million b) £20 million c) £50 million

26 *River City* films a) all year round b) in roughly half a year.

27 The flats on Montego Street are actually fully-kitted out behind the windows of the tenements. True or false?

28 Which member of the cast who played copper PC Harry Black is also one of the main stunt co-ordinators on *River City*?

29 The roads through Shieldinch already existed and had to be built around. True or false?

30 In whose flat is there a piano? a) Scarlett's b) Lenny's c) Malcolm's

For answers, please turn to page 112

Faces From Fiction

Hundreds of actors from home and abroad have ended up in Scotland's soap. Do you know who's who?

1. Angus MacInnes played an American with big ideas in *River City*, after roles in *Eyes Wide Shut* with Tom Cruise and *Witness* with Harrison Ford. What was his character's name in *River City*?

2. Which vindictive woman's character's surname was Corrigan?

3. What is perennial bad man McCabe's first name?

4. Actor Sam Heughan, of Tennent's TV ad fame, played which smarmy character whose namesake is the current British tennis number one?

5. Which longhaired holyman did Irish actor David Murray play?

6. Derek Munn played which cop with a complicated love life?

7. Katie McEwen played Della. But who was Della's husband?

8. Who was Alanna's mum?

9 He played a dodgy schoolteacher by the name of Graeme McDonald, but what was Gordon Kennedy's character better known as?

10 Which tough guy turned up having left the army and was soon starting affairs with women and men – including a reluctant clinch with McCabe?

11 Shirley McDonagh was played by which well-known Scottish actress?

12 Which double barrelled actor plays gangster McCabe?

13 Name the award-winning actress who played his Downs syndrome daughter.

14 Who played Archie Buchanan and his bearded alter ego Douglas?

15 Who played Dr Marcus McKenzie?

16 Cas Harkins played which of Scarlett's brood?

17 He starred in hit film *Sweet Sixteen*, but which character did William Ruane play in *River City*?

18 What was drug dealer JP Walsh's (played by Gary McCormack) Pontiff-themed nickname?

19 Aged just one month Romi Sign was the youngest debutante on the soap when he arrived in 2003 as part of the Rossi family. Who did he play?

20 Which member of the Malik clan did Laxmi Kathuria play? Jamila or Hana?

For More Faces From Fiction,
continue directly on to the next quiz.

For answers, please turn to page 112

More Faces From Fiction

Do you know a Malik from a Murdoch and a Tall Ship barmaid from a Lazy Rays receptionist? Let's see, shall we?

21 Who played Hazel Donachie?

22 Which character did Riz Abassi play?

23 Kirsty Henderson was played by which actress?

24 Which character did Jason Pitt play?

25 Tommy Donachie was the first murder victim in Shieldinch. Who played him? a) Eric Barlow b) Ken Barlow c) Johnny Briggs

26 Joyce Falconer played which Doric tongued quine?

27 Who plays Gina Rossi?

28 Jenni Keenan Green played which flame haired sex bomb?

29 Veteran Scottish acting legend Ida Schuster played which character from the start of the series?

30 Which actor shares his name with the central character in Channel 4's *Shameless*?

31 Lisa Gardner played which character?

32 The façade to the Conway Spices yard still looms over Shieldinch. What's the name of the man it's named after?

33 Patrick Mulvey played Liam McNulty. What nationality is Patrick?

34 Who turned up as a waiter in the country house hotel where the Adams were having the posh Christmas dinner?

35 Garry Sweeney plays which of the Brodie brothers?

36 Who is Christina Michalka's mum?

37 Which country was Christina born in?

38 Which actress plays Stella Walker? a) Keira Lucchesi b) Lorraine McIntosh c) Barbara Rafferty

39 Edinburgh actor Billy McElhaney plays which popular character?

40 Lorna Anderson played which character before leaving in 2011?

For answers, please turn to page 113

Before and After
Montego Street

There is life beyond The Tall Ship, you know. How closely have you followed the careers of those whose CVs include a spell on Scotland's soap?

1 Louise Goodall played Sammy the Snitch's sister Elaine, but which Ken Loach film did she star in?

2 Who went from snogging Shirley in his final Shieldinch clinch to winching Carla Conner in *Corrie* and rubbing shoulders with Kylie in *Dr Who*?

3 Which member of the cast counts *Last of the Mohicans* and *Grafters* as notches on his 40+ year acting CV?

4 Which member of the cast was killed by Joaquin Phoenix in Ridley Scott's *Gladiator*?

5 Which actor joined the cast after establishing himself in *Footballer's Wives*?

6 Which actor, who played latino lothario Luca, starred in the video to Eric Prydz's hit 'Call On Me' and left *River City* to star in *Three* alongside Kelly Brook before also popping up in mega blockbuster *Mamma Mia*?

7 The child actress who played Freya also appeared in the BBC drama *Single Father*, name her. a) Shirley Temple b) Bonnie Langford c) Natasha Watson.

8 When he was starring as a dying man in *River City* which dark haired hunk was also DJ-ing on Real Radio?

9 Which *River City* pensioner was played by a woman whose voice coaching skills have been sought by top Hollywood voice coaching agents?

10 Which singing actress made her acting debut in Ken Loach's *My Name Is Jo* after years of starring in pop videos?

11 Who left *River City* and went on to star in a series of challenges including running a hotel in Tiree, cooking dinner in Glasgow's Gamba for the *River City* cast and being a trawlerman off Barra for the day for BBC Alba?

12 Which *River City* actor was the original co-host of *The Lottery Show* with Anthea Turner?

13 Which long-serving member of the *River City* cast was arrested by eventual *River City* colleague Gray O'Brien in Mark McManus' last ever *Taggart* episode? a) Eileen McCallum b) Johnny Beattie c) Tony Kearney

14 Who starred in a short film *Gas Attack* before landing her part as a nurse in *River City*?

15 Which member of the clinch cast had a small part in the cult flick *The Wicker Man* with Britt Ekland, Christopher Lee and Edward Woodward?

16 Which member of the cast appeared in Ken Loach's racially controversial film *Ae Fond Kiss*?

17 Which former *River City* star's first job after leaving the soap was in *Domino* with Keira Knightley?

18 Which two stars of *River City* appeared in HBO epic *Rome*?

19 Bollywood legend Sayeed Jaffrey had a cameo role in *River City*. True or false?

20 Viewers might have found something familiar about Janette McVey who turned up to take teen temptress Alanna home to Aberdeen, but why?

For a continuation of Before and After Montego Street, proceed directly on to the next quiz.

For answers, please turn to page 113

21 Which *River City* hunk had previously appeared as a regular in *Taggart* as DC Rob Gibson and *Peak Practice* before charming the ladies of Montego Street?

22 Which member of the cast was also an STV prize guy on *Wheel of Fortune*?

23 Which actor also appeared with Cillian Murphy in *The Wind That Shakes The Barley* and opposite Martin Compston in *Sweet Sixteen*?

24 Which blonde *RC* bombshell was a former Armani model?

25 Who featured in Richard Jobson's movie *Sixteen Years of Alcohol* with Kevin McKidd and hedonistic flick *Clube Le Monde*?

26 Who appeared in the famous 'What's It Called? Cumbernauld!' advert on STV in the 1980s?

27 Which Scottish veteran appeared in *Braveheart* as clan Chief Lauchlin? a) Johnny Beattie b) John Murtagh c) Maurice Roeves

28 Which *River City* actor was one of the original cast members of cult Channel 4 comedy *Absolutely*?

29 Who starred alongside Elaine Page in the original cast of *Evita* in London's west end? a) Jo Cameron Brown b) Jenny Ryan c) Libby McArthur

30 Kari Corbett played a junior version of Gillian Anderson's *X-Files* character in a series called *Jeopardy*. True or false?

For answers, please turn to page 113

Montego Street Music Makers

Glasgow is a UNESCO City Of Music, so it's no surprise to find that music plays a big role in the lives of many of the actors, and the characters themselves. It's the music round. So pin your ears back.

1. What connects the incidental music of *Pearl Harbour*, *Hanibal*, *Gladiator*, *Terminator* and, er, *Sportscene*, with the opening credits of *River City*?

2. Which ginger haired member of the cast featured in the 2003 series of BBC talent show *Fame Academy*?

3. Which *River City* actress knocked Madonna off the top of the album charts in 1989 with her band's LP 'When The World Knows Your Name'?

4. Which *River City* character, who played gangster JP, played drums with Scots punk act The Exploited (who famously had their dole money stopped when they were spotted in 1981 singing on *Top of The Pops*)?

5. Susanne Bonner is a well-known Scottish jazz singer, but what character did she play in *River City*?

6. Eddi Reader guested as Gina and Eileen's cousin in 2008. True or false?

7 What's the connection between the soap and the band who scored a number thirteen hit with a cover version of The Mamas and The Papas' hit single 'California Dreamin'' in 1990?

8 Which Fife actress, whose character Yvonne is an occasional returning character, is also a director/radio DJ and recording artist, having supported The Cranberries, Radiohead and Blur, and also recording with Arab Strap?

9 Which actor played in Glasgow bands Eryka and Merchant City during his time at *River City*?

10 Which automobile-themed 1970s disco classic did the cast get together to record a video for BBC's Children In Need?

11 Which member of the Shieldinch cast performed a song in an episode of the soap that he had originally penned in the hope that Susan Boyle would record it?

12 Who connects Horse, Mylo, Eddi Reader, Carol Laula and Michelle McManus to *River City* musically?

13 Legendary Scottish blues singer Tam White played which member of the Mullen clan?

14 Glasgow's Gospel Truth Choir teamed up with the cast of *River City* to release a charity version of a Paolo Nutini single. Which one?

15 Which oddly nick-named character busked outside the underground, singing a Crowded House cover version on his guitar?

16 Which member of the cast had a hit in 1980s with 'Don't It Make You Feel Good'?

17 Which *River City* pair performed as Eurovision pop act hopefuls City Chix in 2006?

18 Did they make it through to represent Britain?

19 Which female character was the singer with Drew and Big Bob's band in 2010?

20 Name the song Big Bob sang in an episode of the soap which actor Tom Urie then released as a single.

For answers, please turn to page 114

Real Life Beyond the River

Of course, *River City* is all fiction. But some of the lives of the actors who bring the drama to life have been every bit as interesting as their characters'. How much do you know?

1. Name the *River City* hairdresser who has been cutting hair in real life for three decades before landing the part in the soap.

2. Which real life nurse became a nurse in the soap?

3. Ryan Smith plays Charlie in *River City* but in real life what does his brother Darren do?

4. Which former member of the cast was at the centre of a medical emergency when he suffered a heart attack in his pal's car on the M8?

5. What connection did the characters of councillor Alex Judd and Sharon McLaren have off-screen?

6. Which infamous real life pair did some speculate Daniel and Marianne McKee's characters might have been based on, or have been loosely inspired by?

7. Which member of the Murdoch clan is a trained masseuse in real life and was sometimes called on to rub co-stars' aches and pains away?

8 Which cast member was the victim of an unprovoked attack in a Glasgow bar and needed facial reconstruction?

9 Which actor was given an MBE in the Queen's Honours List in 2007.

10 Which Doric *River City* favourite was formerly a kiss-o-gram?

11 Which actress represented Scotland at the Special Olympics in Glasgow?

12 Where did actor Juan Pablo Di Pace, who played Luca, come from?

13 Whose role as a gay cop was a case of art imitating real life from his pre-acting days?

14 Which young ginger haired actor was hospitalised after a scene with an iron bar went slightly wrong?

15 Who previously sold pies and Bovril to the fans at Aberdeen's Pittodrie stadium?

16 Which actor who played a fatherly figure on Montego Street had former employment as a bouncer at one of London's most infamous strip clubs?

17 Which actress unsuccessfully stood for rector at Glasgow University?

18 What is Gilly Gilchrist's real name? a) Gilbert b) Gilfillan c) Gareth

19 Who was celebrating their Fiftieth year in Scottish show business when the show started in 2001?

20 Which member of the cast has worked as a clown doctor in hospitals across Scotland? a) Carmen Pieraccini b) Johnny Beattie c) Ida Schuster

For answers, please turn to page 114

Two Bob Job

They're two of the most lovable characters in the soap, so they get a category all to themselves. Are you well-versed in the ways of the Bobs? Let's see.

1. Why did Shellsuit Bob pretend to Roisin that he had lost the power of his legs after coming out of a coma?

2. When Shellsuit was in a coma, Scarlett used something other than smelling salts to waft under his nose, telling him to 'breathe it in'. What was it?

3. How did Shellsuit end up in a coma?

4. What's the name of Shellsuit Bob's garage?

5. Where did Bob book his honeymoon for he and Charlie? Cairngorms or Chicago?

6. When Shellsuit proposed to Zara what Proclaimers song was he singing?

7. Which other bloke did Shellsuit Bob share the caravan with?

8. Big Bob works where?

9 Big Bob dressed as an olive to do a promotional day for The Tall Ship. What did he dress up as when he was doing a promotional day for a local pizza parlour?

10 Who enlisted Bob's help to make an emergency wedding cake after she knocks one over in the deli hours before it's due to be delivered?

For answers, please turn to page 115

Raymondo's Tall Ship
General Knowledge Pub Quiz

Get the drinks in and make sure you get me a packet of dry roasted. It's pub quiz time ...

1 When BBC Scotland showed the first episode of *River City*, STV were showing Manchester United in the Champions League. Who won the viewing figures contest?

2 Which sci-fi film character was Vader nick-named after and why?

3 Which Rangers-daft actor plays a Celtic-daft sportsgear-wearing ex-ned?

4 Which blonde-haired character, in the early days, had ambitions to become a night-club singer?

5 If you were betting on *River City* in 2003 in the bookies what would have been betting on? a) a greyhound b) a racehorse c) a pop band

6 The Oyster Café is based on the retro cafes around Scotland such as Jaconelli's, University Cafe in Glasgow and The Ritz in Millport, but which country is that design associated with?

7 Which character was passed over for the lead parts in *Sweet Sixteen* and *Ratcatcher* and was on the verge of turning his back on acting before landing the part of one of the most popular characters in the soap?

8 Who was the lynchpin of the Save The Doocot campaign in 2002?

9 Which street name connects Shieldinch to Jamaica?

10 Which blonde haired lady character initially harboured ambitions to sing semi-professionally?

11 When Raymond said 'I'll give it a year, max' in the first episode he was referring to a) the soap's expected tenure b) the length of time before the papers started slagging it off c) the expected duration of Eileen and Tommy's marriage.

12 He stashed his stepsister's clothes and installed a spy camera in her room. Who's this weirdo?

13 Who went from floral-print dresses to moody sullen goth after her boyfriend dumped her?

14 Which gay character comes from Stornoway?

15 Which Muslim character started wearing a headscarf after her interest in religion grew, but worried how it would go down with the Shieldinchers?

16 Who took Raymond to the cleaners during a poker match in 2003, cleaning him out of his savings?

17 When she was trapped inside the den made by creepy Brian Henderson, a rat that had the same name as one of her Doric-speaking neighbours kept Hazel company. Was it called? a) Roland b) Rizzo c) Roisin

18 Which sportswear-clad character was merely a bit part player in *River City's* original format – but became a key figure and remains one of the most popular?

19 Kieron Elliott briefly played a gay bit-part character who had a fling with Scott in the soap's first year before later turning up as Heather Bellshaw's ex Duncan Robertson in the series. True or false?

20 Tam Dean Byrne, who plays baldy gangster McCabe, once went on a poetry tour with rebel rocker Pete Doherty. True or false?

For a continuation of Raymondo's Tall Ship General Knowledge Pub Quiz, proceed directly on to the next quiz.

For answers, please turn to page 115

The pub quiz competition always picks up after the break.
Who'll win the top prize of a hamper from The Montego
Deli and a cheese toastie at the Oyster Café?

21 Julie Coombe played Terri Johnstone. But why did Scarlett hate her?

22 What did Daniel Schutzmann and Lorraine Kelly's entrance scenes have in common, location wise?

23 What does it say on the massive warehouse that looms over Montego Street?

24 Which pair of women old enough to know better once had a food fight in the deli?

25 The hairdressers was originally known as Moda Vida. What does Moda Vida actually translate as?

26 What was the cliffhanger storyline to mark the fifth anniversary show?

27 Why did Jimmy get out of his taxi on the fateful day he was run over by joyriders?

28 Where did Fi bolt to when she thought she'd driven Archie to kill himself?

29 How many kids did bubbly hairdresser Viv have away from Shieldinch?

30 Who stepped in as a fortune teller when Zelda the Magnificent failed to show up at the Shieldinch Easter fete?

31 Which pensioner set up a short-lived writing group?

32 Which of the student trio of Charlie, Innes and Jennifer turned out to be gay?

33 Which Shieldinch granny took in an asylum seeker called Makenba after reading an advert in a magazine in 2009?

34 Comedienne Janey Godley played which of the following characters in a short appearance in the soap? a) dodgy mechanic b) dodgy landlady c) dodgy psychic

35 When Liz collapsed ahead of the Shieldinch Christmas show, which old dame stepped in to save the show?

36 What was the name of the short film that Innes and Charlie submitted to the Shieldinch short film project? a) Mystic River City b) Bonnie On The Clyde c) The Shieldinch Witch Project

37 When the Shieldinch community centre was trashed, which pensioner did CCTV footage reveal to be the unlikely culprit?

38 Why were Robbie and Hayley so shocked when they realised they'd spent a night in bed together fuelled by alcohol?

39 What did Jennfier discover about the private life of the old woman who died in the flat next door and lay undiscovered?

40 Ruth has had three surnames. What are they?

41 What did Raymond do to baby Stewart's Christening gown before his Christening ceremony?

42 Who helped alcoholic lesbian Fi after she got trapped behind the wheel of her car and was being goaded by Archie?

43 Which *RC* actor famously lost out to Brandon Routh in the battle to become Superman in Bryan Singer's mega blockbuster *Superman Returns*?

44 Whose 40th birthday was it in episode one?

45 The tenements on Montego Street were once inhabited. True or false?

46 What is special about the date Tuesday, 24 September 2002 in *River City*'s history?

47 George Henderson once paid his alcoholic daughter to leave her son Deek with them and go to London to sort out her demons. True or false?

48 Whose silence did Fraser Crozier buy after dumping toxic waste on an area of land in order to make it cheaper to buy?

49 What do the characters Jo Rossi, Lenny Murdoch and Kelly Marie Adams have in common?

50 Gina formerly worked on a cruise ship – which of her daughters did she fall pregnant with there?

For answers, please turn to page 115

ANSWERS

RIVER CITY PEOPLE

1. Una McLean
2. Grayson
3. Fraser Crozier
4. a) politician
5. Paddy Adams. Theresa had an affair with her sister's man.
6. Sam Robertson
7. Robbie Fraser
8. Brian McCardie
9. He has been one of the writers.
10. He played hard man Daniel McKee.
11. c) Marianne
12. Charlie Drummond
13. a) Lawyer Fi
14. Louise Jamieson
15. An undercover cop called Beth Logan sent to clear up behind DI Whiteside
16. Paul and Jamie Hunter
17. b) lawyer
18. Shona McIntyre
19. Michael Nardone
20. Tina Hunter

MORE FROM MONTEGO STREET

1. Allison McKenzie and Lisa Gardner
2. Franco Rossi
3. Joan Burnie
4. c) Drummond
5. Gordon McCorkell
6. Stephen Purdon
7. To see his sister Kelly Marie in Peru
8. Sally Howitt
9. Libby McArthur
10. Paul Samson

CLYDESIDE COUPLING

1. a) cherry picker
2. Michelle
3. Scarlett and Kelly Marie
4. Tina
5. Iona
6. Jack
7. Amber and Jennifer
8. Liz
9. She burst in *Graduate* style and disturbed the nuptials.
10. That she was 14
11. Iraq
12. d) Scott
13. Ukraine

14. At a music festival
15. Hannah
16. Nicole Brodie
17. PC Harry Black
18. True
19. True
20. False

MORE CLYDESIDE COUPLING

21. Big Bob and Iona
22. c) Nathan
23. He was pretending to be the biological father of Ruth's baby.
24. Jamie Hunter
25. Kelly Marie
26. Father Michael
27. Hooker Zoe
28. Heather Bellshaw
29. Nicki
30. Sonny
31. True
32. Liam
33. Jimmy
34. Niamh
35. Lesbian lawyer Fi
36. Her foster father and teacher Mac
37. Alanna
38. Jo Rossi
39. Scott Wallace
40. Alice Henderson

CLYDESIDE COUPLING CONTINUED . . .

41. Heather Bellshaw
42. True, in 2003
43. Lewis Cope
44. Mac
45. Deek's dad Mac
46. Hazel
47. Lewis Cope
48. Cormac O'Sullivan
49. Nazir Malik
50. Tommy Donachie
51. Lewis Cope
52. Yes, just before George died of a brain tumour
53. Niamh Corrigan
54. Iona
55. Leyla
56. Charlie Bowie
57. Annie Sobacz
58. Because Jack was her dad Gordon's best mate
59. True and Shona had a miscarriage due to the stress.
60. A divorce

CLYDESIDE CRIME

1. Prof Michael Learmonth
2. He picked up an undercover cop working as a prostitute.
3. He stole charity money to help clear his debts.
4. Daniel McKee

5. He ran him over in a hit and run.
6. He made his sister drive the car away while he stayed to help.
7. Sharon McLaren from Arran
8. Archie Buchanan
9. Prestwick Airport
10. Embezzlement
11. His brother Robert
12. Four (after she'd married Raymond for the first time)
13. Detective Chief Inspector
14. Irish firebrand Niamh Corrigan
15. He went undercover as part of a sting.
16. Zoe
17. Billy Davies
18. Roisin
19. Joyriders ran him over
20. Nicki and Shirley

MORE CLYDESIDE CRIME

21. Robert Henderson
22. Malcolm
23. c) 500
24. McCabe
25. He was trying to help settle his family debt with McCabe.
26. Barlinnie
27. Gina, Ruth and Heather
28. Malcolm
29. Heather Bellshaw
30. Jo Rossi

31. Jo Rossi
32. He kidnapped her and held her hostage.
33. Cormac
34. George Henderson
35. Cormac O'Sullivan
36. Paul Hunter
37. Vader
38. Jo Rossi
39. Nicki Mullen
40. He tried to buy her silence.

SIBLINGS IN THE CITY

1. Roisin, Shona and Iona
2. Madonna, Bob (sort of) Kelly Marie and Stevie
3. Iona
4. Leo, Michael and Gabriel
5. Michael, Gabriel and Leo
6. Conor and Nicole (Adeeb is only his step son)
7. Roisin and Shona
8. Paul and Jamie Hunter
9. Eileen
10. Robert
11. Stevie Adams
12. He bedded Jo while he was seeing Ruth.
13. Malcolm Hamilton
14. Zara
15. d) none of the above
16. Gina
17. Yes, a brother Robbie in Manchester
18. Archie

19. Half sisters. Ruth's the product of a fling, and Jo is Franco's daughter.
20. Leo

SOAPY DOUBLES

1. Stefan Denis
2. Tony Kearney
3. b) Mamta Kash
4. Libby McArthur's Gina Rossi
5. c) *Casualty*
6. *EastEnders*
7. *Crossroads*
8. Fran(ces) Healy
9. Queen Vic barmaid Lorraine Wicks
10. Kari Corbett
11. Gray O'Brien
12. Rosi Di Marco, matriarch of the dodgy Di Marco clan
13. They both played Adam Barlow in *Coronation Street*.
14. *Brookside*
15. Allison McKenzie
16. They both fell to their deaths from rooftops.
17. Gray O'Brien
18. *Coronation Street*
19. Deepak Verma
20. *High Road*

FAMILY TIES

Clan Murdoch

1. Lenny
2. His ex-wife Mary, their son Ewan and Archie Buchanan
3. Dodgy moonshine vodka
4. b) marine
5. Charlie Drummond
6. Lenny and Shellsuit Bob
7. McCabe's daughter Donna
8. Father Michael
9. Lenny Murdoch
10. Amber
11. Lenny
12. True
13. Lee
14. Lenny
15. None. He was a stand-alone character initially.
16. English. He was brought up down south by his mother.
17. c) clothing boutique
18. True. Lenny returned mid-2011 and Amber left later in the year.
19. A 4X4 with blackened out windows
20. a) Hamish

Clan Rossi

1. Ruth
2. Great grandson

3. They got up to rumpy pumpy in the radio studio and accidentally broadcast their interlude when one of them flicked a switch they shouldn't have.
4. Jo
5. Andy Carroll
6. Ruth
7. The Lake District
8. True
9. Dubai
10. Glasgow Central Station
11. Eilidh
12. Scott
13. Italy
14. She handed him a leaflet about syphilis inside a Valentine's card before throwing his clothes out of the window.
15. Her sister Jo
16. Adam Khan
17. Australia
18. Lucky Jo Rossi
19. Jo with Cormac
20. Hamilton

8. A scratch on his neck from his previous victim
9. Sister
10. Cornton Vale's Women's Prison
11. Half sister
12. Cousin
13. He pulled on a stag do and caught an STD.
14. Oban
15. O'Hara
16. Jimmy and Scarlett argued – Jimmy thought she fancied the prof and that the prof fancied her.
17. Shellsuit Bob
18. Alfie
19. Shellsuit Bob
20. They had a win on the horses.
21. Jimmy
22. First Floor
23. He was mown down by neds joyriding.
24. She'd had her power cut off for not paying the lecky bill.
25. Dad

The Adams Family

1. Bubba
2. Monaco
3. Her mum Scarlett
4. Shellsuit Bob
5. Molly
6. Big Bob
7. Big Bob

ARRIVALS & DEPARTURES

1. Canada
2. Madonna Mullen
3. Christmas Day
4. He pulled up in a black stretch limo.
5. Tommy Donachie
6. c) 'The wedding's aff.'

7. Gray O'Brien's character Billy Davies
8. Zoe
9. Billy Davies
10. Alice Henderson
11. a) 810,000
12. The builders renovating The Tall Ship had gone into liquidation and vanished.
13. He found out Ruth had had their baby and not an abortion – and came back to claim the kid.
14. The Shieldinch rooftops
15. Andrew Murray
16. Glasgow Central
17. Lake District
18. Shellsuit, Gina, Malcolm, Eileen, Deek, Raymond (Argument mediator's note: Shellsuit was in the cast from the start but was only an 'extra' originally)
19. She was bribed with £10,000 by Lenny to get out of Rory's life, but he wanted to come with her so she staged a fake clinch with Ewan to make him hate her.
20. London
21. Italy
22. Brian Henderson
23. London
24. Subway
25. His sister Kelly Marie

MONTEGO STREET MARRIAGES

1. Jo Rossi
2. George Henderson
3. She stuffed sausage rolls into her handbag.
4. The second
5. Italy
6. She watched a video of Scarlett and Jimmy's wedding, on which there was a heated exchange between Archie and Liz.
7. Food poisoning (Carmen Pierracini had, in reality, left the show.)
8. Her. But he'd already said he didn't love her.
9. Las Vegas
10. They were tied up to the Shieldinch fountain.
11. Gina
12. Tony (played by Phil McKee)
13. c) 'Sunshine on Leith' by Proclaimers
14. There is no church on Montego Street.
15. c) 'Young Hearts Run Free' by Candi Staton
16. Ross Minto
17. a) Loch Fyne
18. A Vegas-style one
19. Scott
20. Alanna

CHRISTMAS ON CLYDESIDE

1. Her son Archie
2. Jimmy hid the tot's presents in the oven and Scarlett put the oven on.
3. c) in a taxi
4. c) 'When You Wish Upon a Star'
5. In the loo at The Tall Ship
6. Raymond Henderson
7. Roisin
8. Drink alcohol
9. Scarlett
10. George Henderson

SHIELDINCH PUBLIC HEALTH DEPARTMENT

1. Innes Maitland
2. Malcolm
3. a) Australia
4. The doctor left out her files accidentally on purpose and surgery cleaner Molly found them.
5. Ruth Rossi
6. True
7. Deek pushed him down the stairs after Bob slept with his mum.
8. He suffered a stroke after collapsing.
9. A specialist neurological rehabilitation centre
10. Ruth

11. Paul Hunter – he couldn't cope with his dad being gay.
12. She was caught in the blast at the caravan that killed nasty Alex.
13. His sister Alesha Shah
14. Ruth – her own daughter
15. Alice Henderson
16. Roisin
17. Shirley
18. Marijuana
19. Malcolm
20. Brian Henderson

MORE MEDICAL MATTERS

21. Lewis Cope
22. HIV
23. True
24. Stella Walker
25. Leyla Brodie
26. Her son Deek
27. Jimmy Mullen
28. Scarlett
29. Fi Kydd
30. A brain tumour

YOU CAN CHOOSE YOUR FRIENDS, BUT NOT YOUR FAMILY

1. Eight years
2. Lee
3. Big Bob is Shellsuit's uncle
4. Her mum Tricia

5. Because he was a religious minister from Lewis, he had strong religious beliefs about homosexuality and refused to accept Scott's kidney because he was gay.
6. Theresa
7. Sister
8. She's their half sister.
9. She's his cousin.
10. Murray
11. Maurice Roeves
12. By doping her with sleeping tablets
13. She discovered he wasn't her real dad.
14. Robert, his brother
15. Her son Deek
16. Aberdeen
17. She couldn't cope with the prospect of killing her son (even though she hadn't).
18. Eileen and Gina
19. Liz
20. The urn containing her late husband's ashes

RELATIVE VALUES

21. Stepmum
22. Conor
23. Nephew
24. Because Brian's dad is Deek's mum's brother
25. Jimmy Mullen
26. Iraq
27. Stepdaughter-in-law
28. That Eileen was pregnant to Raymond after a one-night-stand
29. Paddy Adams – he had a fling with Theresa.
30. Stevie Adams

GUEST APPEARANCES

1. Lorraine Kelly
2. He played a nude model at life drawing classes.
3. Allan Russell
4. Tony Roper
5. Hannah Gordon
6. Brian 'Limmy' Limond
7. Scott Mills
8. Ronald Villiers, played by Ford Kiernan
9. False
10. a) Billy Davies

LIFE BEYOND SHIELDINCH

1. David Murray aka Father Michael
2. Tony Kearney
3. Tony Kearney
4. *The Karen Dunbar Show*
5. Michale Nardone and Maurice Roeves
6. Colin McCredie
7. Jayd Johnson
8. *Tinsel Town*
9. Anthony Martin
10. Barbara Rafferty
11. Ewan Stewart

12. Tony Kearney
13. Frank Gallagher
14. *True Blood*
15. *Bergerac*
16. b) Leela
17. Chris Brasier
18. Tom Urie
19. *High Times*
20. Michael Nardone

SHIP SHAPE

1. Gordon
2. Big Bob
3. d) Liz Buchanan
4. True. He bought it in 2008 after Sharon left Raymond bankrupt after taking a loan off Lenny.
5. Jimmy and Scarlett
6. The Grill
7. She claimed she was pregnant.
8. a) Six
9. Blue
10. b) Four

PARENTHOOD

1. Roisin
2. Lewis Cope
3. He was infertile.
4. Deek
5. Mac the schoolteacher
6. Shirley
7. Lewis
8. Billy and Della

9. Olivia
10. Nicki and Zoe
11. Sixteen
12. Malcolm
13. Malcolm
14. Raymond
15. Mary Murdoch
16. True
17. False
18. Stepmum
19. Three
20. Luca

A SHIELDINCH STROLL

1. On the site of the former Versus wine bar
2. Fraser
3. Just Gordon
4. Malcolm
5. a) 20 Montego Street
6. c) 22 Montego Street
7. a) Chinese take away
8. Scarlett & Co
9. a) 5
10. Ruth & Scott
11. Lazy Rays and the former solicitor's office
12. Conway Spices
13. The Malik family
14. A) opposite the Oyster Café
15. Fountain
16. False. There's one right next to the fountain.
17. Yes, next to the health centre
18. True

19. Blue
20. Gold

MORE AROUND MONTEGO . . .

21. Bells Bridge
22. The Glenlee, harboured at the riverside Transport Museum, is known to Glaswegians as The Tall Ship, also the name of the pub in *River City*.
23. b) Four
24. a) choice malts and fine ales
25. a) The Clyde Enquirer
26. a) ferry
27. a) The Ferry Inn, Renfrew
28. The Tall Ship
29. a) Paton's Lane
30. The secluded archway next to the Montego Deli
31. a) cigarettes and ices
32. A big ice cream cone
33. The basketball court
34. Green
35. Molly
36. At his late wife's graveside
37. Andy
38. Victor
39. At the bottom of the stairs up to Scarlett's flat
40. Upstairs at The Tall Ship

MOVING ON TO A BETTER PLACE

1. Her son Franco and his father Nazir
2. They've all died in off-screen storylines.
3. Because she was supposed to go to the airport to pick them up but went to a life drawing class instead. They got a taxi that crashed.
4. Jimmy had to reluctantly have him put down.
5. Archie and Mary, Lenny's ex-wife
6. Archie was killed by one of Lenny's henchmen.
7. Their old neighbour Iris
8. She was killed in London by a hit and run driver.
9. Her grandson Brian Henderson
10. She had a brain tumour.
11. That he took control of The Tall Ship from Lenny again
12. On Barra in the Western Isles
13. Ewan Murdoch
14. A brain tumour
15. Lenny Murdoch – although we never actually saw him do it and he had never been convicted of the crime
16. Archie Buchanan

17. Lenny Murdoch stabbed him.
18. She was killed in a car crash in Cardiff.
19. She broke her neck after driving drunk and crashing the car.
20. Amber

DISPATCHES ON THE BANKS OF THE CLYDE

21. He died in an explosion in the caravan when he left the gas on and lit up a fag.
22. Jo Rossi
23. Heather Bellshaw
24. Tommy Donachie
25. With a spanner
26. Her son Deek
27. No. When they filmed the identification scene there was just a green sheet over a body. No sign of Alice.
28. His hand moved
29. Brian Henderson – he's the only one who has left but isn't dead (yet).
30. False. George hasn't made an appearance since he died . . . so far.

WORKING NINE TO FIVE

1. Jimmy Mullen
2. a) an arts student
3. Shrink
4. The Grill
5. Nicki
6. Dancing
7. Lydia Murdoch
8. Med Dreams
9. a) a lawyer's firm
10. Gerry and Fi
11. True
12. a) a fast food joint
13. She was a cleaner.
14. In the deli
15. Della's mum Shirley
16. Professional footballer
17. Livingston FC
18. Deekafe
19. Shellsuit Bob
20. An estate agent

SHIELDINCH INDUSTRIES LTD

21. Versus
22. He was a postman.
23. She was a hairdresser.
24. Shirley
25. Alanna
26. Archie Buchanan
27. a) graphic designer
28. Roisin
29. He was a cabbie.
30. Serge
31. Nazir Malik
32. Blink Inc.
33. His late parents
34. Daniel McKee
35. The roof collapsed.
36. Sonny
37. Charlie Bowie

38. Murray
39. Gabriel Brodie
40. Eileen

BEHIND THE SCENES AT SHIELDINCH

1. *High Times*
2. *Stookie*
3. It went from two half-hour episodes to one hour-long episode a week.
4. Jason Merrells
5. A photograph of him appeared in a book.
6. a) cream cheese – ice cream melts under the lights
7. Lena Martell, but the BBC flat-out denied it
8. Stephen Greenhorn
9. George Henderson
10. Rod Stewart
11. c) abseil
12. b) cola
13. c) concrete and plaster
14. c) plastic
15. True, sort of, it's alcohol free
16. Two crews working on different scenes at the same time
17. The first ever omnibus episode
18. b) Lorne Balfe
19. *Sunshine on Leith* featuring The Proclaimers' music
20. a) J&B whisky bottling plant

MAKING MONTEGO STREET

21. a) 194,000. It now enjoys a respectable 500,000 regularly.
22. a) Dumbarton
23. Varnish
24. They're all filmed on the same plot of land in the Dumbarton BBC studios compound.
25. a) £10 million
26. b) in roughly half a year
27. False. Most of the interior scenes are filmed in replicas built inside one of the former warehouses.
28. Carter Ferguson
29. False. The buildings you see on set were built from scratch to fit the purpose.
30. c) Malcolm's

FACES FROM FICTION

1. Sonny
2. Niamh
3. Thomas
4. Andrew Murray
5. Father Michael Royston
6. DCI Eddie Hunter
7. Billy Davies
8. Roisin
9. Mac
10. Stevie Adams
11. Barbara Rafferty
12. Tam Dean Byrne

13. Paula Sage
14. Gilly Gilchrist
15. Aussie star Stefan Denis.
16. Stevie
17. Troubled Brian Henderson.
18. The Pope
19. Franco
20. Jamila

MORE FACES FROM FICTION

21. Anne Marie Fulton
22. Nazir Malik
23. Kari Corbett
24. Chef and ex con Cormac O'Sullivan
25. a) Eric Barlow
26. Roisin McIntyre
27. Libby McArthur
28. Heather Bellshaw
29. Lily Fraser
30. Frank Gallagher
31. Jo Rossi (the second)
32. The late Thomas Conway
33. American
34. Douglas aka Archie
35. Gabriel
36. Tatiana
37. Ukraine
38. a) Keira Lucchesi
39. Jimmy Mullen
40. Amber Murdoch

BEFORE AND AFTER MONTEGO STREET

1. *My Name is Joe*

2. Gray O'Brien
3. Maurice Roeves
4. Gilly Gilchrist
5. Daniel Schutsmann who played Marty Green
6. Juan Pablo Di Pace
7. c) Natasha Watson
8. Kieron Elliott
9. Jo Cameron Brown
10. Lorraine McIntosh
11. Tony Kearrney
12. Gordon Kennedy
13. c) Tony Kearney (bonus point to anyone who noted that Tom Urie was also a bouncer in this episode)
14. Morag Calder
15. Barbara Rafferty
16. Shabana Bakhsh
17. Riz Abbasi
18. Michael Nardone and Gilly Gilchrist
19. True, he played sexist surgeon Ishwar Shah.
20. She was the star of the famous Scottish Blend TV adverts, Aileen Mowatt.

BEFORE AND AFTER MONTEGO STREET CONTINUED . . .

21. Gray O'Brien
22. Tony Kearney
23. William Ruane
24. Allison McKenzie
25. Allison McKenzie

113

26. Morag Calder who played Ruth
27. b) John Murtagh
28. Gordon Kennedy
29. a) Jo Cameron Brown
30. True

MONTEGO STREET MUSIC MAKERS

1. All were worked on or written by Scottish composer Lorne Balfe.
2. Ryan 'Vader' Fletcher
3. Lorraine McIntosh of Deacon Blue
4. Gary McCormack
5. Lola Fraser
6. False
7. The band are called River City People.
8. Cora Bissett
9. Ryan Fletcher
10. 'Car Wash' by Rose Royce
11. Tom Urie performed 'Never Been Kissed' as Big Bob.
12. They've all recorded or performed with Tom Urie.
13. Jimmy Mullen's dad Kid
14. 'Last Request'
15. Vader
16. Stefan Denis
17. Jade Lezar and Laura McMonagle
18. No, Daz Sampson did.
19. Iona
20. 'Never Been Kissed'

REAL LIFE BEYOND THE RIVER

1. John Comerford
2. Ruth Rossi played by Morag Calder
3. He's a professional footballer.
4. John Murtagh
5. They are real life brother and sister, Brian and Sarah McCardie.
6. Jimmy Boyle and now ex-wife Sarah Trevelyan who was a therapist Boyle met during his time at Barlinnie (but, of course, the soap's NOT based on any person, living or dead etc etc)
7. Chris Brasier
8. Michael Nardone
9. Johnny Beattie (He joked it stood for Mr Beattie Entertainer.)
10. Joyce Falconer
11. Paula Sage
12. Argentina
13. Derek Munn aka Eddie Hunter
14. William Ruane
15. Joyce Falconer
16. John Murtagh – he worked at London's Nell Gwynne strip club.
17. Jenni Keenan Greene
18. c) Gareth
19. Johnny Beattie
20. a) Carmen Pieraccini

TWO BOB JOB

1. Because he was trying to con her into giving him some of her lottery winnings
2. A poke of chips
3. Deek pushed him down a flight of stairs.
4. Montego Motors
5. Cairngorms
6. Sunshine On Leith
7. Deek
8. In the ticket office at Shieldinch tube station
9. A tomato
10. Iona

RAYMONDO'S TALL SHIP GENERAL KNOWLEDGE PUB QUIZ

1. River City did, with over 800,000 viewers to Champion's League's 400,000 in Scotland
2. Darth Vader from the *Star Wars* films on account of the fact that he had asthma
3. Stephen Purdon
4. Jo Rossi
5. a) a racehorse that had the same name as the soap
6. Italy
7. Stephen Purdon
8. Malcolm
9. Montego Street is named after Montego Bay in Jamaica, a throwback to Glasgow's heritage as a city that traded with the West Indies.
10. Jo Rossi
11. c) the expected duration of Eileen and Tommy's marriage
12. Brian Henderson
13. Kirsty Henderson
14. Scott Wallace
15. Zara Malik
16. Billy Davies
17. c) Roisin
18. Shellsuit Bob
19. True
20. True, they toured Russia together in the mid 2000s.

RAYMONDO'S TALL SHIP GENERAL KNOWLEDGE PUB QUIZ CONTINUED ...

21. Because Terri bullied her at school
22. They were both made at Shieldinch underground station.
23. Conway Spices
24. Roisin and Gina
25. Life fashion
26. Archie was pushed over the cliff by his wife and her accomplices.

27. He swerved to avoid a woman with a pram, hit a bollard and got out to inspect the damage.
28. Millport
29. Two
30. Iona
31. Liz
32. Jennifer
33. Shirley
34. c) dodgy psychic
35. Malcolm, aka Johnny Beattie veteran of many a Christmas panto
36. c) The Shieldinch Witch Project
37. Molly in her mobility buggy
38. Robbie is gay.
39. That she was gay and had lived all her life in secret
40. Green, Carroll and Rossi
41. He spilled tomato sauce down it.
42. Deek
43. Sam Heughan aka Andrew Murray
44. Hana Malik
45. False
46. The first episode of *River City* was shown
47. True
48. Deek's
49. They've all left and returned to Shieldinch.
50. Ruth, her first born

RIVER CITY SCORESHEET

Under 50 points:
It's called *River City*. It's on BBC Scotland. Has been for years. You've been watching *Emmerdale* instead, haven't you? Sort it out or McCabe will be round.

50–100 points:
You've been sitting next to an avid *River City* fan at work/in the living room for years and have consumed information about the show without even realising you're doing it. You probably feel a bit violated. Either give in to it or get your desk moved/divorced.

100–300 points:
You have long-term memory problems. The scriptwriters will love you for this as you don't remember half the storylines that were abandoned without conclusion. What happened to Carly and Lola? Dunno? Neither does anyone else, really.

300–500 points:
You're an undergraduate at the University of Shieldinch, on course for a solid 2:1 in soap frippery.

Over 500 points:
You've a PhD in the Social, Economic, Criminal, Moral and Philosophical Imperatives of Shieldinch. You're a Montego Street master, the Shieldinch Sensei, the Yoda down the road from Yoker. Congratulations. Help yourself to one of Gina's buns.